~Views of Old~
PLYMOUTH

Sarah Foot

Bossiney Books

D1451579

First published in 1983
by Bossiney Books
St Teath, Bodmin, Cornwall
Designed, typeset and printed in Great Britain by
Penwell Ltd, Parkwood, Callington
Cornwall
All rights reserved

ISBN 0 906456 72 X

To my son Charles
who loves Plymouth as his great
grandfather did before him.

Acknowledgements

I am greatly indebted to my cousin Stanley Goodman
who read my manuscript and told me many stories of
Plymouth, the city where he has lived and worked all his
life and about which he is a mine of information.

Most of the photographs were supplied by the
Plymouth City Museum and the Local History Library,
where the staff were consistently helpful and informative
and where I spent many a happy hour leafing through
their comprehensive collections of photographs of the
city.

I am also grateful to Mrs Joyce Law who lent some
unique old postcards of Plymouth which have added on
extra dimension to the book and to Dermot FitzGerald
for his second-world-war photographs. The photograph
of the return of Sir Francis Chichester was generously
provided by the *Western Morning News,* Drake's Drum
by Robert Chapman, and the cover colouring is by
Paul Honeywill.

And finally, a lot of the credit must go to Brenda
Duxbury who not only edited the book but was
responsible for the lay-out and encouraged me with her
great enthusiasm throughout.

Bibliography

Plymouth—A New History Vols I, II, Crispin Gill, David
and Charles
Plymouth—A Concise History, Tom Gant, Baron Jay
Ltd.
A History of Plymouth, C.W. Bracken, S.R. Publishers
Ltd.

**The following photographs were supplied by
Plymouth City Museum:** 5, 9-15, 17, 23-25 (*upper,
centre*), 26, 27, 32, 33, 36, 37, 40, 41 (*upper*),
42-44, 46-48 (*upper*), 51 (*lower*), 52, 54, 56-58
(*lower*), 60, 61 (*lower*), 62 (*lower*), 63 (*lower*), 64, 65,
68, 69, 71, 72, 74, 75, 77, 78 (*lower*), 79 (*upper*),
80-85 (*upper*), 86 (*lower*), 87, 89, 95-101, 109, 116,
118, 119, back cover.

ABOUT THE AUTHOR—AND THE BOOK

Sarah Foot lives at St Mellion, Near Callington. Formerly on the staff of the *London Evening News,* she contributes regularly to the *Western Morning News.* This is her sixth title for Bossiney. In 1981 she wrote the text for *Views of Old Cornwall,* an immediate best seller, and she is currently working on *The Cornish Countryside.* Sarah Foot's previous titles were *My Grandfather Issac Foot, Following the Tamar,* and *Following the River Fowey.*

Here in Views of Old Plymouth words and old pictures combine to recall Plymouth as it once was. 'This was the town from which the Pilgrim Fathers sailed for the New World,' she writes 'where Cookworthy made the first English porcelain, and where the people held out for the Commonwealth against the Royalists in the Great Siege of Plymouth which lasted for three terrible years.'

Sir Francis Drake, Sir Walter Raleigh, Robert Falcon Scott and Nancy Astor are only some of the characters who people the pages. Many of the old buildings inside these pages have long since gone but, as the author puts it, 'I hope this collection of old photographs of the city will be a reminder of those great times past and of the spirit of the people of Plymouth—a spirit that lives on.' A valuable addition to the library of Plymouth—and for all who love the city.

~Views of Old~
PLYMOUTH

Plymouth has a special place in the hearts of many people. It has been home to great sailors and explorers, to fishermen and artists, to trading people and merchants, to landowners and engineers. Its history is long and complex and full of pageantry. I hope this collection of old photographs of the city will be a reminder of those great times past and of the spirit of the people of Plymouth—a spirit that lives on.

Plymouth began as a port and for many years was known as Sutton, that being the first development of the town. And Plymouth still remains, primarily, a town of seagoing and sea-loving people, so that its character seems to be moulded by the sea and those with seafaring occupations.

Once the city was known as the Three Towns. Devonport, Stonehouse and Plymouth were administered separately until as recently as 1914 when the amalgamation took place.

It is a city of views, partly because it is built on hills, but also because of the fine sea vistas, in particular from the Hoe across the wide sweep of Plymouth Sound with Drake's Island and the man-made breakwater to the inscrutable horizon beyond.

The Hoe has long been part of Plymouth's history for legend tells us Brutus, who had arrived at Totnes with a party of Trojans, organised a wrestling match between one of his champions and the Giant Gogmagog who resisted Brutus and his army.

The contest took place on Plymouth Hoe and it was a long hard fight but finally the Trojan, Corineus, managed to throw the giant to the ground by his girdle and then flung him over the cliff. The sea was said to be stained with his blood for days after.

For hundreds of years there was a figure of the giant carved out of the turf on the Hoe in memory of the battle. It was only with the building of the Citadel in 1666 that all traces of the figure disappeared.

From Trojans and Saxons, then the French and the Bretons, to the famous Spanish Armada and King Charles's men, armies have come to Plymouth. Sailing below the cliffs to threaten the town, they had many a bloody battle. But the staunchness of the Plymothians remained undefeated.

During Elizabethan days Plymouth was the most important seaport in England and many great adventurers and explorers set sail from here for far off lands. In fact, over the centuries many Plymothians saw the coast of America but never travelled as far as Exeter. They explored by sea but not by land.

It is impossible to appreciate fully the essence of Plymouth without knowing and feeling the historical connotations. So many great men have walked these streets, so many high dramas have taken place in and around the city.

My grandfather, Isaac Foot, who was born in Notte Street, was always in love with the city and brought its history alive to us as children. 'Along

In 1936 a half-size replica of Drake's famous flagship, the *Golden Hinde,* had a trial trip around Plymouth Sound in preparation for the approaching Naval Week. The ship is giving a practice broadside from her half-size guns, loaded with powder as they were in the original fifteenth-century vessel (right).

4

A Newman print of Plymouth: the Laira,
Cattewater and Sound looking from Efford.

that street', he would say referring to his birthplace, 'must have walked Humphrey Gilbert, Sir John Hawkins, Sir Francis Drake, Martin Frobisher, Sir Walter Raleigh, Admiral Robert Blake and in later years Captain Cook and Admiral Nelson.' Then he would take us up on the Hoe and tell us the stirring story of Francis Drake finishing his game of bowls while he kept the Spanish Armada waiting.

This was the town from which the Pilgrim Fathers sailed for the New World, where Cookworthy made the first English porcelain, and where the people held out for the Commonwealth against the Royalists in the Great Siege of Plymouth which lasted for three terrible years. Even when their food and water supplies were cut off the people did not give in.

It was here in later years the famous explorer Robert Falcon Scott was born in 1868 and Nancy Astor was to become the first woman Member of Parliament to take her seat in Britain. My grandfather was her Liberal opponent in the election of 1919 in Sutton, Plymouth.

And when the German bombers came in the last terrible attack on Plymouth in the Second World War they very nearly wiped out the city; flattening hundreds of buildings and claiming over a thousand civilian lives. The number of servicemen lost was never released. But once again the spirit of Plymothians proved indomitable. After the raids, the people of Plymouth would gather on the Hoe to dance.

This was the second summer of the war;
yet every night, sedately,
most innocent and stately,
the boys and girls were dancing,
were dancing on the Hoe.

(Clemence Dane)

Now Plymouth has been rebuilt and has many modern buildings of which to be proud, including the grand new Theatre Royal opened in 1982. But sadly many of the old buildings that had not been obliterated by the bombing were later pulled down to make way for new construction.

Many people regret the passing of some of the beautiful old Jacobean and Elizabethan buildings. They feel that despite the cost and trouble they should have been preserved. Fortunately many of the Elizabethan buildings on the Barbican were saved by a group called the Plymouth Barbican Association. In 1957 they set up an appeal fund to

At the Declaration of the Plymouth Division
by-election November 1919 Lady Nancy Astor
became the first woman MP in Britain.
She took her seat on 1 December 1919. She
won the by-election with a majority of 5,000
votes over T.W. Gray and Isaac Foot who can
be seen standing second from the right on
the rostrum.

save and restore the houses in New Street which the City Council were threatening to demolish. But for them we would have lost the last great remnants of Elizabethan Plymouth.

So the Plymouth that Leland described as 'This towne about King Henry the 2 tyme was a mene thing as an Inhabitation for the Fischars and after increased by a litle and a litle', has done just that and more. Maybe it is because Plymouth has known so many hardships that the people of this city bear an almost fanatical allegiance to their home. It is this allegiance that gives the city its heart.

Below: Old houses in Southside Street on the Barbican.
Right: Palace Court—a picture taken before 1878.

Earlier views of three gates of Plymouth.
Above: Old Town Gate. Right: Hoe Gate.
Below: Frankfort Gate.

Old Town Gate (above) and Frankfort Gate
as they were in the latter part of the
nineteenth century.

The children of Jago's School, Coburg
Street, in 1890. At this time I believe my
grandfather, Isaac Foot, was a pupil at this
school.

Right: Plymouth High School for Boys first
opened in 1878 and then amalgamated with
Mannamead School in 1896 to become
Plymouth College. It is still going strong.
The boys appear to be wearing a variety of
clothes: straw boaters, sailor suits, plus
fours and caps.

Left: The Turk's Head Inn is believed to be Plymouth's oldest inn and it stood at the corner of Higher Lane where it entered St Andrew's Street. It was demolished in 1865.
Below: Passage House Inn at Cattedown, Plymouth, which no longer exists but is a typical example of Plymouth architecture.
Right: The Old Ring of Bells in Woolster Street.

The Elizabethan House is one of the restored buildings in New Street. It is open to the public and has been carefully furnished with period pieces and has a most interesting pole staircase made from an old ship's mast. The house is reminiscent of the sixteenth century when this area of Plymouth was thriving with activity.

The entrance to old Plymouth Castle from Lambhay Street in 1892. The fortification was probably built in the fourteenth century and was strengthened and restored several times in Plymouth's history to guard against the French and the Spanish. The Castle was prominent in the siege of Plymouth during the Civil War.

Prince Maurice

HIS WARRANT

Since the Raiſing of the Siege.

To the Conſtables of *Egbuckland*; and after notice taken of Publiſhing, To the Conſtables or Tythingmen of St. *Budeaux*, there to be Publiſhed.

FOr as much as divers perſons diſaffected to his Majeſties ſervice, make their daily recourſe into Plymouth, furniſhing the Rebels there with all manner of proviſion for Man and Horſe, contrary to his Majeſties Proclamation, prohibiting the ſame : theſe are therefore ſignifying, That if any perſon of what degree or quality, doe ever preſume to have any commerce or dealing with any in the ſaid Towne of Plymouth, or otherwiſe; ſend into the ſaid Towne, or take, or carry with him any

D 2   Horſes

The Siege of Plymouth: Part of the Siege Warrant posted by Prince Maurice. Prince Maurice arrived on the scene of the Siege in September 1643 with five regiments of horse and nine of foot. He made his headquarters at Widey. He was actively involved in the Sabbath Battle of Freedom Fields on 3 December of that same year. But his demands for a surrender were only answered with renewed fighting from the townsmen of Plymouth who eventually defeated the Royalist forces.

Two of the designs for windows at the Plymouth Club depicting scenes from the Siege of Plymouth 1643-45. The club in Lockyer Street was destroyed in the blitz of the second world war.

One picture (opposite) shows the women courageously bringing strong waters to the men and the other (left) shows King Charles I summoning the town to surrender.

Plymouth stood out against the Royalist forces for over three years and their bravery and endurance has become one of the legends of the city.

It was many years before Plymouth recovered from her prolonged resistance and it was estimated there were nearly 8,000 deaths during the Siege, more than the entire population of the town.

Above: A drawing by Sir Bernard Gomme, the engineer who built the Citadel in 1666, taken from his plans. (Reproduced by permission of the National Maritime Museum).
Left: Royal Citadel Gate.

The Citadel Gateway (below left) attributed to Thomas Fitz, is said to be one of the nation's finest examples of baroque architecture. The Citadel was built in 1666 on the sight of the former fort for which Drake and Hawkins were responsible.

Though the Citadel was built for the defence of Plymouth, Charles II's mistrust of the people was shown in that the guns could, if necessary, be used against the town. The King, it was felt, had not forgotten that the people of Plymouth held out against the Royalist Forces for three long years.

The question has often been asked why the niche at the top of the gateway is empty and many believe that a statue of Charles II was originally planned to be erected there.

A print of Plymouth showing the outline of the Citadel.

The Guildhall which was opened by the Prince of Wales in 1874.

The earliest Guildhall in Plymouth was built in the fifteenth century. In 1606 the Jacobean Guildhall was built. In the hall was room for a prison, a court, and below vegetable markets. In 1800 the Jacobean Guildhall was removed and the New Guildhall was built. In 1874 the present Guildhall was opened but later badly damaged by the air raids of the second world war.

The opening of the Guildhall on 13 August
1874 by the Prince of Wales, later Edward
VII. It was a great occasion for Plymouth and
as can be seen by the photograph thousands
of people attended the ceremony.

It was said that the Prince was handed a
grand silver key with which to open the
Guildhall doors, but try as he could the key
would not turn. Eventually the doors were
opened from within.

Left: The laying of the Foundation Stone of
the 'New Guildhall' in 1870. Norman and
Hine were the architects and Mr John
Pethick the builder. Mr Pethick was Mayor of
Plymouth from 1898-1900.

St Andrew's Church, the Mother Church of Plymouth, which was badly bombed during the war. A place of worship has stood on this ground since Norman times when the Augustinian Priory of Plympton served the chapel here. The oldest part of the present church dates from the fourteenth century and in 1460 Thomas Yogge, who was three times Mayor of Plymouth, paid for the tower to be built.

When the church was bombed during the war the outside walls were not too badly damaged. The inside was cleared and laid out as a garden and the services in this garden church became part of Plymouth life. Nailed to the entrance of the church after the bombing was a placard reading, 'Resurgam' (I will arise again). And so it has been proved. The rebuilding of the church started in 1949 when the Queen, then Princess Elizabeth, laid a stone commemorating the beginning of the restoration. On St Andrew's Day 1957 the church was reconsecrated for public worship by the Bishop of Exeter in the presence of HRH Princess Alice, Countess of Athlone.

In the picture we also see the Prysten House, a fifteenth-century building, and the Old Workhouse which was built in the seventeenth century and was originally called the Hospital of the Poor's Portion.

2036 Plymouth: Abbey Gate.

This building has three names: Yogge's House after the man who was said to have built it; Plymouth Abbey for this is where monks from the Plympton Priory were first said to have housed a holy order in Plymouth; and Prysten House meaning Priest's House. It has been damaged and restored several times over the years but we are lucky that so much of the original building still remains even after the siege and wars that Plymouth has known since the time when it was built.

A beautiful piece of carving on an old Georgian panel that was part of the front door of the original St Andrew's Vicarage which was demolished in 1868. The Vicarage once stood where the present General Post Office now stands in Westwell Street. This panel dates from 1460.

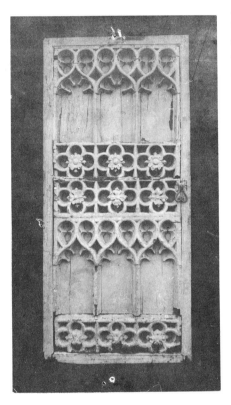

The Hospital of the Poor's Portion in Catherine Street, now demolished.

Left: Almshouses above Catherine Street.
Below: The Old Almshouses at the corner of Ham and Green Streets which were founded in 1674 and demolished in 1868.

Plymouth's Old Workhouse with St Andrew's
Church rising behind. On this site the
Guildhall was eventually built.

Sir Francis Drake is probably the most famous of all Plymouth's heroes. The very sound of his name brings forth a galaxy of stories from the past of bravery and adventure and good deeds. He was Mayor of Plymouth in 1581-82 and by his 'energy, influence and purse brought in the waters of the Mew (Meavy) to provide for the needs of Plymouth'. Until then the water for the city came mostly from wells.

But of course he is best known for the way he dealt with the Spanish Armarda. The two

paintings illustrate parts of the famous story. The one above right shows Drake continuing his game of bowls, determined to finish before he dealt with the Spanish fleet; the other (above) shows Don Pedro de Valdez surrendering his sword to Sir Francis Drake on board the *Revenge* during the attack of the Spanish Armada. Both paintings are by J. Seymour Lucas.

The engraving (below right) shows the English Fleet and the Spanish Invincible Armada off Start Point near Plymouth.

He was playing at Plymouth a rubber of bowls
When the great Armada came;
But he said 'They must wait their turn good souls',
And he stooped and finished the game.

(Newbolt)

A View of the Engagement between the English Fleet, and the Spanish Invincible Armada off the Start Point near Plymouth

Drake's Drum which is now in safe keeping at Sir Francis Drake's home Buckland Abbey.

Drake he was a Devon man an' ruled the Devon seas
(Captain art thou sleepin' there below?)
Rovin' tho' his death fell, he went wi' heart of ease,
An' dreamin' arl the time of Plymouth Hoe
'Take my drum to England, hang it by the shore
Strike it when your powder's runnin' low
If the Dons sight Devon, I'll quit the port of Heaven
And drum them up the Channel as we drumm'd them long ago.
(Newbolt)

Francis Drake's brother, Thomas, brought the great drum back from Drake's last voyage in the *Defiance* when he died of dysentry and was buried at sea along the Panama coast.

The picture below shows a mural which hangs in Buckland Abbey, once the home of Sir Francis Drake. It depicts the running battle as the English harried the Spaniards up the Channel. After the Spanish Armada was defeated by the English fleet a big storm scattered the Spaniards and sunk most of their ships. A medal was struck at the time of the victory with the Latin words which translated mean 'He blew with His winds and they were scattered'.

Sutton Pool in the days when sailing barges
set the scene.

Plymouth Regatta, an occasion for ships to
dress overall and every kind of seagoing
vessel to appear on show from rowing boats
to warships. The first Plymouth Regatta was
held in 1827 and soon after this the Royal
Western Yacht Club opened.

Sutton Pool, Coxside.

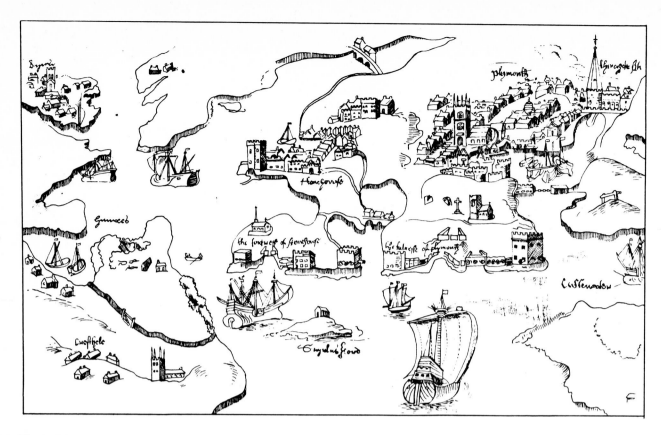

Henry VIII's map of Plymouth. At this time
Plymouth was just becoming one of the
major ports of England.

There are still remains of three of the forts
built at this time and the one at Devil's Point
is still well preserved and is at the present
time being converted into a restaurant.

Plymouth Dock in 1785. It was in 1691 that
the dock in the Hamoaze was first begun.
During the eighteenth century much building
took place not only of the docks themselves
but of the houses around. The workmen for
the dockyard were originally housed afloat
but in the first thirty years of the eighteenth
century six streets of houses were built and a
terrace of officers' houses. By the end of the
century the town's population was half as
large again as that of Plymouth itself.

The Royal William Victualling Yard at Stonehouse built between 1824 and 1835 by Sir John Rennie at a total cost of £700,000. Said to be one of the most outstanding engineer-designed buildings in the country it covers 14 acres of land and a statue of King William IV still stands on the grand entrance gate. Note the paddle steamer in the foreground, so popular in the last century which took visitors up the Tamar River.

The Royal Naval Barracks built by the famous engineer John Jackson between 1898 and 1903 when there was a huge building boom in Plymouth. Before the barracks were built seamen were housed in old hulks in the Hamoaze.

John Jackson was knighted later when he finished building the Manchester Ship Canal. He was responsible for dock buildings all over the world. He became a Unionist MP for Devonport and lived at Pound House, Peverell.

In 1941 the Barracks were severely damaged during the worst week of bombing in Plymouth. It was not until 1970 that the Royal Naval Barracks was extensively modernised and new blocks were added.

Commandant's House, staff quarters and the new buildings of the Royal Marine Barracks at Plymouth. When the Marine force was raised in 1755 the Plymouth Division was billeted around Sutton Harbour and later men were housed out in many outlying districts. The new building for the Marine Barracks was built on land bought from Lord Edgcumbe and was first occupied in 1783. It was added to in 1857. The railings which separated the original parade ground from Barrack Street disappeared with the Victorian extension.

Raglan Barracks which was built in 1854 and named after the Commander in the Crimean War. It was the beginning of many new fortifications for the town of Plymouth. Only a few years later, when the ambitions of Napoleon III were alarming the British government, Plymouth was to be surrounded by forts. Bovisand, Breakwater, Picklecombe, Tregantle at Whitesand Bay, Scaresdon and many others were built from 1860 onwards. Raglan Barracks was demolished in 1969.

William Cookworthy, the discoverer of the commercial use of china clay and the inventor and maker of Plymouth porcelain. There are some fine examples of Cookworthy's porcelain in the Plymouth Museum. He was born at Kingsbridge in 1705 and died in 1780 having achieved worldwide fame, not only for his porcelain but as a scholar and a scientist.

Captain James Cook, 1728-1779, who made three historic voyages of discovery from Plymouth. In 1768 he sailed in the *Endeavour* for his first circumnavigation of the world; in 1772 he left for New Zealand in the *Resolution* and again in 1776 but this was to be the last time. He was never to return as in 1779 he met his death at the hands of natives in Owhyhee.

Sir Martin Frobisher, 1535-94, the great explorer who discovered the North West Passage. Later he sailed with Drake to the West Indies and he was knighted for his part in the Armada defeat. He died at Plymouth of wounds received while attacking Brest, then in Spanish hands. It was said of Frobisher: 'His highest ideal was courage, tempered by piracy.'

Sir John Hawkins, another great sea captain of the sixteenth century, who sailed to the Canary Islands, the West Indies and Florida and is said to have introduced tobacco and potatoes to England. His father was a great merchant of Plymouth and his brother was also a sea captain and explorer. He sailed on many voyages with Drake against the Spanish and was Comptroller of the Queen's Navy for twenty-one years from 1573. He was born in 1532 and died at the age of sixty three.

One of Plymouth's ancient inns,
the Rose and Crown, in Old
Town Street, Plymouth.

A view of Old Town
Street looking towards
Drake Circus.

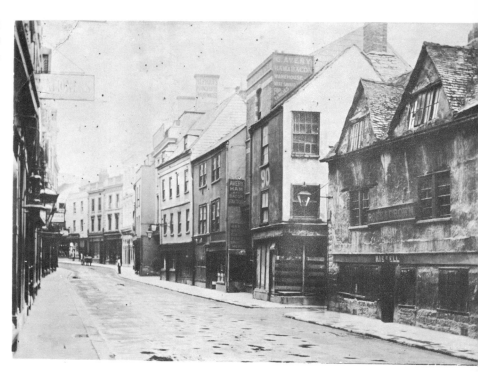

Old Four Castles Inn
in Old Town Street.

The Globe Hotel: The lower photograph shows a coach pulled by ten grey horses leaving the Globe Hotel in the early part of this century. These coaches were soon to be replaced by trams and buses.

The Globe Hotel was once a humble tavern but after 1800 it became one of the most famous coaching centres and later the political headquarters of the Conservative Party.

The upper picture, taken in the early part of this century, shows the inside of the famous Globe Restaurant.

Globe Hotel
and
Borough Arms

The unveiling of the Rooker Memorial in
Guildhall Square. When the new workhouse
was built in 1849 the corporation of
Plymouth bought the old site to build a
Guildhall. The Liberal Alderman, Alfred
Rooker, was behind the scheme, but it was
many years, not until 1873, that the Guildhall
was opened by the Prince of Wales. A statue
was erected to Rooker's honour by the side
of the municipal buildings but it was
destroyed by bombing in 1941. Drake was
the only other Mayor of Plymouth who was
honoured in the same way.

Palace Court in a picture taken before 1879.
This building was once one of the finest
examples of domestic architecture in
Plymouth. Some feel that it must have
been a religious house but more often it is
said to be the home of one John Paynter who
was a rich merchant of the city and five times
Mayor. It was in this house that Catherine of
Aragon was said to have spent a fortnight in
1501 after her arrival at The Barbican when
she came to marry Henry VII's eldest son.

Later the house belonged to the Trelawny
family and then it deteriorated into a slum
dwelling let out to 'as many miserable people
as could be crowded into its miserable
rooms'. In 1880 the historic house was
removed to make room for a school and
today only a portion of wall remains.

A view of Saltash from the Devon banks. You
can see the paddle steamer heading up the
Tamar and the ferry that ploughed to and fro
for centuries. The rail and road bridges
which now span this stretch of water have
greatly altered this view.

Saltash on the Tamar

Two old views of Plymouth. The one below shows the Exeter Road coming towards the old town at Seven Trees and the one above the horse ferry crossing to Mount Edgcumbe under sail at the mouth of the Hamoaze.

45

A group photograph with all the props.
Horses and carts, buckets, milk churns,
babies and hats and pinafores. Taken about
1900 at Tollox Place, Plymouth, in the Laira
district.

Camel's Head at Plymouth in more rural
days. The name Camel is said to derive from
Kemyll who was the large landowner in the
district in Edward I's reign.

Old Houses at King's Brewery, Notte Street.
Nearby lived the great china man of
Plymouth, Cookworthy. This street was, in
the sixteenth century, one of the most
important in Plymouth. It was almost totally
demolished during the last war.
Right: Pin Lane looking down into Southside
Street. These houses were demolished in
1898.

Houses in Basket Street at the beginning of
this century in a complete state of disrepair.
They later made way for the Municipal
Buildings, which were bombed out in the
blitz of the Second World War.

High Street, Plymouth in 1880.

Looe Street, Plymouth in 1895.

The Winter Villa was built by the Earl of Mount Edgcumbe at Stonehouse in 1856 because his Countess could not endure the winters at Mount Edgcumbe and the Cremyll crossing was so dangerous during the winter months.

My great grandfather, Isaac Foot, owned the house for sometime and it was sold to the Catholic Sisters as an orphanage at the time of his death in 1927. The nuns renamed the building Nazareth House.

It was demolished in October 1976 and a modern building was erected on the site as an old people's home and a small orphanage.

Fore Street and Catherine Street Devonport, when the streets were far busier with pedestrians and the horse and cart than they are now with motor traffic.

Mountwise from Devonport column with sailing ships in the harbour in the last century. All these houses were bombed in the blitz and have since been replaced by blocks of flats.

**Michael Foot canvassing in Devonport during
the 1950 election.**

There were paddle steamers on the Tamar
from 1839 onwards. New companies with
steam paddle boats were opening almost
every year until 1895 and doing very good
business both in transporting goods and
taking passengers on pleasure jaunts.

The *Princess Royal* steaming under the Royal
Albert Bridge, the famous railway bridge
built by Brunel.

The Barbican: At the Barbican Fish Quay (above and right) huge fleets of fishing boats came in to unload their catch. In 1896 the quay was widened to accommodate the fishing industry.

The entrance to the harbour at the Barbican.

A ship's chandler on the Barbican
in the last century.

Two fine views of Plymouth Hoe (below and below right) showing the pier and Smeaton's Lighthouse. Originally built in 1759 on Eddystone Reef, which is one of the most dangerous reefs in the British Channel, the Smeaton tower replaced Winstanley's Lighthouse and Rudyerd's which had been built there before. The first disappeared in 1703 in one of the worst storms ever known, the second was destroyed by fire. Smeaton's Lighthouse lasted one hundred and twenty three years guiding hundreds of ships safely past the treacherous reef. It was finally removed to the Hoe when the rock on which it stood was found to be undermined by the sea.

The Hoe & Pier, Plymouth. W 7682.

EDDYSTONE LIGHTHOUSE, PLYMOUTH

Douglas's Tower. The fourth Eddystone
Lighthouse built in 1890. The stump of John
Smeaton's Tower is shown on the left.

The public shelter on The Hoe.

Plymouth Hoe when ladies wore long dresses, hats and gloves and were sheltered from the breezes and the sunshine by elegant parasols. Here people sat, as they do today and have since time immemorial, and gazed at the uplifting view of the great Plymouth Sound with Drake's Island and beyond. Once the great sailing ships came and went; and now the Roscoff ferry, the warships and the tankers pass to and fro.

The Hoe with Smeaton's Tower and the bandstand.

From Victorian times one of the main
features of the Hoe was the elaborately
designed pier which was destroyed in the
blitz. Built in 1884 it was a distinctive
landmark with its domes, wrought iron
railings and clock.

In 1812 the mammoth task of building Plymouth Breakwater was begun. Plymouth harbour had long been considered dangerous because it was open to the full force of south-westerly gales and it was hoped that by building the breakwater these dangers would be halved.

But it was a major task and once again John Rennie the famous engineer was asked to produce plans. He worked alongside John Whidbey, a Naval officer.

Over a mile long, it was constructed of local limestone and faced and paved with granite with a lighthouse on the western end. The completion of this great breakwater made Plymouth Sound one of the safest and finest harbours in the world. Nearly 3½ million tons of stone was used in the making and several times the storms altered the angle of the wall. Finally the builders decided to leave the slope at the one in five angle which the sea kept reducing it to, and so the incline of the breakwater was eventually dictated by the elements. Although work had begun in 1812 it was not finished until 1844 when the lighthouse was first lit.

A view of Cattewater from the Citadel. In 1809 Lord Boringdon from Saltram was responsible for laying mooring chains in the Cattewater and by 1815 there were six shipbuilders there. With other shipbuilders in Sutton Pool and the Hamoaze there were twenty to thirty vessels built each year in Plymouth in the early part of the nineteenth century and in 1880 Cattewater was handling a huge amount of trade from all over the world.

Hulks in the Hamoaze in 1905.

Mutley Plain where the Royal Eye Infirmary
was situated. The Infirmary began its life in
Cornwall Street in 1821 and was founded by
Dr J. Butter and Dr E. Moore. Dr Butter was
referred to as the 'beloved physician' and
served the infirmary for thirty two years.
Below: A steam train arriving at Mutley Plain
Station.

Halfpenny Gate, Stonehouse.

In the early years of this century trams
dominated the roads of Plymouth. A view of
Mutley Plain left and Halfpenny Gate,
Stonehouse, above.

In March 1891 there was a most ferocious
blizzard and snow storm in and around
Plymouth. These photographs were taken at
that time. They show Derry's Clock (above
left), always a central landmark of the town;
Athenaeum Street (left) and (above) parkland
at Mount Edgcumbe.

The damage done to trees and buildings
was obviously most substantial.

Cremyll, near Devonport

Cremyll, near Devonport where the old sea
crossing from Mount Edgcumbe used to
arrive.

Beechwood Cottage on the Mount Edgcumbe
estate.

70

Mount Edgcumbe viewed from Mount Wise.

Camel's Head bridge, Plymouth, built in
1902. Devonport and District Tramway
Company built a line from Morice Square to
Saltash Passage but the old wooden bridge
at Camel's Head was not strong enough to
carry the trams and people had to disembark
on one side and walk to the other until the
new Camel's Head Bridge was finished.

Paddling at Mount Batten beach when ladies
wore long dresses and boaters and no
gentleman was ever seen outdoors without a
hat.

Lower: Plymouth Fire Brigade in 1890.
Upper:Devonport Fire Brigade in 1904.

74

Diamond Jubilee celebrations of the
Stonehouse Police and Fire Brigade in 1897.
Those were the days when these festivities
were taken seriously and it is rather
marvellous to see how each window and
balcony and pointed roof is carefully and
exotically decorated with flags and banners,
ribbons and plants. The buildings and the
dress of the people in the photograph belong
to a lost age and so does the atmosphere it
conjures up in our minds.

Some great occasions in Plymouth's History:
1. The Victoria Record Reign Celebration in Plymouth which took place on 22 June 1897.

The timber for the huge bonfire, said to be the largest of many such bonfires built for this occasion, was brought from the slum clearance at Looe Street.

Apparently when the bonfire was lit hundreds of lice and fleas escaped from the timbers and caused much discomfort to the local dignitaries who were positioned in the enclosure nearby. Many had to leave the ceremony and make for home unable to bear the consequent itching!

2. The steam train which brought Edward VII and Queen Alexandra to Plymouth during their Westcountry tour in 1902. This was the first time a Great Western Railway Royal train was to run from Plymouth to Paddington via Bristol. The decorated engine was named Britannia especially for the occasion.

3. The Grand Opening of the Palace Theatre, Plymouth on 25 September 1911. The theatre originally opened in 1898 and in 1911 Tommy Hoyle became the famous extrovert owner. His widow was to keep the music hall going right through World War II and most of the well-known variety acts appeared there.

30.9.13
S.J

MAYFLOWER
1620

On the 6th of September, 1620, in the Mayoralty of Thomas Townes after being "kindly entertained and courteously used by divers friends there dwelling" the Pilgrim Fathers sailed from Plymouth in the Mayflower, in the Providence of God to settle in NEW PLYMOUTH, and to lay the Foundation of the NEW ENGLAND STATES ∾ The ancient Cawsey whence they embarked was destroyed not many years afterwards, but the Site of their Embarkation is marked by the Stone bearing the name of the MAYFLOWER in the pavement of the adjacent Pier This Tablet was erected in the Mayoralty of J.T. Bond 1891 to commemorate their Departure and the visit to Plymouth in July of that Year of a number of their Descendants and Representatives

4. The Prince of Wales landing in Plymouth from *Renown* in June 1922. Alderman Pearse, Chairman of the East Stonehouse District Council, is seen receiving HRH after his Eastern Tour.

5.   A celebration to mark the alterations to the Mayflower steps in 1934. These steps mark the point on the Barbican where the first band of Pilgrim Fathers left Plymouth and sailed for America. Their reason for leaving England was so that they might have a higher degree of freedom in worship than they had been allowed in England at that time. They left Plymouth on 6 September 1620, though they had originally sailed from Southampton, having come into Plymouth because the ship needed repairs. Crew and passengers were received kindly in Plymouth and offered hospitality until they sailed, eventually landing in Plymouth, Massachusetts, which had been so named by Captain John Smith. They landed on 20 December which Americans still celebrate as Forefather's Day. Above left: The original plaque on the wall at the Barbican.
Right: The new monument at the Mayflower Steps.

MAYFLOWER 1620

Plymouth, Devon, England

Mr and Mrs William Snell of Wellsbourne
House, Hartley Avenue, Plymouth at one of
the outings they arranged for convalescent
servicemen during the First World War.
Friends would come with their cars to take
the men out for drives. Here they are outside
Wellsbourne House in 1917.

Some recruits for Kitchener's Army in
Plymouth, September 1914.

The Royal Sailors' Rest in Devonport. Miss
Agnes Weston, whose mother was of the
Plymouth Bayly family, came to Plymouth in
1873 working for the temperance movement
amongst the sailors. Three years later she
opened the Sailors' Rest in Devonport. This
picture was taken before the erection of the
Jubilee Wing and the south extension.

Miss Agnes became known as the Sailors'
Friend and later Queen Victoria was to make
her a Dame. Her idea was to give the sailors
a 'public house without a drink'. The finished
building was capable of housing 900 people.

Charles Church before it was so severely bombed during the last war. Now it is a war memorial for the city and stands in its gutted state amidst the busy traffic. The building of this church was started just before the Civil War and was not completed until 1658. It is named after King Charles I who gave permission for the church to be built. Until that time St Andrews was the only church in Plymouth.

The handsome edifice of the Wesleyan Chapel in Ham Street, now known as Ebrington Street. The large building was designed by the architect H.J. Snell and was built in 1897 with galleries and a sizeable organ in the elegant interior. It was gutted by fire in 1937. The gutted building was partly restored and used for some years as a restaurant but it was completely demolished in 1960.

2034 Plymouth: Charles Church.

Above: Frankfort Street showing Kerswell's
Leather Warehouse which appears to be
moving to Old Town Street and Drake Street.
Left: The Plymouth Co-operative Society's
Headquarters built in 1894 at the bottom of
Frankfort Street.
Below: The Royal Hotel and St Andrew's
Chapel and Terrace.

Left: The staff of Wills and Co. of Union Street are all on parade to have their photograph taken.
Below: Early days of trades unions. The Amalgamated Society of Tailors and Kindred Workers making their point with all the family joining in.

Plymouth/Lee Moor Tramway: Loaded trucks
could run downhill at speed (above) and
were then drawn by horses near Laira
towards the goods yard (below).

The Reservoir, Tavistock Road, Plymouth. It was Drake who first saw to it that Plymouth should have a plentiful source of water and brought a leat to Plymouth from the River Meavy. The Burrator Reservoir is just an extension of the original plan. Town reservoirs were built in Tavistock Road and North Road in the 1820s.

A fine view from the Citadel over the roof-tops of Plymouth. This was taken in 1919 and, although so many of the buildings have disappeared or changed, this is still one of the finest views of Plymouth.

The Chinese Bell, Mount Wise, Devonport. This ancient Bell, said to be over 900 years old, was found in an ancient temple at San-hai-Kwan by the crew of the cruiser *Pique* in 1903. When the ship returned to Plymouth the crew presented the bell, which weighs over 1900 cwt, to the Commander Sir Edward Seymour, and it was hung in front of Admiralty House.

The South Devon and East Cornwall Hospital which was built on its present site in 1884. At the time it was neighbour to a prison and a workhouse and known by the local people as 'The Mutley Mansions'. Now Plymouth has a brand new hospital at Derriford but the move from Greenbank and Freedom Fields has only partially taken place. Sir Massey Lopes of Maristow, who had been MP for South Devon for twenty years, gave generously to the hospital, £14,000 between 1891 and 1899. When the hospital first opened it accommodated 124 in-patients, but by 1928 the in-patients numbered 2,415. In that same year HRH Princess Mary, Viscountess Lascelles, laid the foundation stone for an extension.

Plymouth Argyle team in 1903-1904. It was
this year that a professional football team
was formed called Plymouth Argyle. The
name appears to have come from the fact
that a few soccer enthusiasts had gathered in
a house in Argyle Street to arrange and
discuss the formation of an athletic club.
This was in the year 1888. The Argyle
athletic club was one of the earliest soccer
clubs to be formed in Plymouth, as until that
time this had been a rugby stronghold.

Mr Sam Rendell who is a great expert on the history of Plymouth Argyle was able to tell me all about this match played between Plymouth Argyle and Norwich City at Home Park on 2 September 1905.

It was the opening game of the season for Argyle and was the start of their third season as a professional club.

There was a crowd of 7,000 to see the game and both sides had player managers. The Argyle player manager was the famous Mr Robert Jack who had taken over from Argyle's first manager Mr Frank Brettell.

Argyle won the match by two goals to nil. In the photograph the Argyle side are the club in dark jerseys. Their colours were green jerseys, black collars and cuffs and white shorts. The Norwich colours were described as canary and green jerseys with white shorts. The Norwich club's nickname is the 'Canaries' and at one time their ground was always known as 'The Nest'.

The grandstand shown in the photograph was a wooden structure and was there when the Argyle Athletic Club took over the ground in 1901. It remained until 1930 when it was replaced with a fine structure which was destroyed during the blitz. The present stand is the third at Home Park.

The blitzed grandstand at Home Park
in 1941.

Plymouth Argyle v Luton Town. Home Park
on 10 January 1948 3rd Round FA Cup. The
attendance was 40,000.

The day that the FA Cup came to Home Park
in 1950: Wolverhampton Wanderers, who
had won the Cup the previous year, paraded
it before the match, but they were held to a
draw on this occasion in the 3rd round.

The Prince of Wales in Plymouth in 1919 listening to Mr R. Maunder, who wore a medal showing that he was a sailor on the *Revenge* which escorted Queen Alexander when she came to England for her wedding.

The Lord Mayor of Plymouth, Mr H.M. Medland, reading the notice of proclamation of King Edward VIII from the steps of the Municipal building 1936.

The unveiling of the Door of Unity at St
Andrew's Church, Plymouth, 30 May 1930.

This marks the story of a young Captain of
the USN Brig *Argus* who died when the ship
was in action in the channel with HMS
Pelican in 1813. The Captain, and the body
of one of his dead officers, was brought
ashore at Plymouth and when the Captain
died the two were buried in St Andrew's with
signal marks of respect and regret. A
memorial stone which reads 'Here Sleep the
Brave' was placed between St Andrew's and
the Prysten House. During the late 1920s the
American Society of the Daughters of 1812
provided for the restoration of the doorway
from the churchyard to the Prysten House as
a memorial to the chivalrous act of the
British people so long ago. On May 30 1930
the dedication was performed by the Lord
Bishop of Exeter. Mrs Harper D. Sheppard
was the Chairman, at that time, of the
American Society.

The original memorial stone was mounted
beside the doorway and a service is still held
each year which is attended by American
residents and visitors as well as local people.

Left: Isaac Foot and Nancy Astor
campaigning during the 1919 election.
Although they were political opponents they
were to become life-long friends. Nancy
Astor won the seat for the Conservatives at
this election and she then became the first
woman to take her seat in the House of
Commons.

Nancy Astor canvassing for the 1919 election
outside the Clare Buildings, Coxside.

Undaunted by the terrible air raids of 1941 Plymothians would meet on the Hoe to dance in the evenings. It was a practice started by Lady Nancy Astor and below right she is seen dancing with one of the sailors. The other picture shows part of a typical crowd of servicemen and civilians who danced with gay abandon and a sort of defiance which helped to boost morale throughout the city.

Mr George Bernard Shaw who came to open Astor Hall, Plymouth in October 1929 at the invitation of Lord and Lady Astor. The Astors were trying to encourage a university with colleges at Exeter, Plymouth and Redruth and Astor Hall was to be the first hall of residence. Twenty years later the University opened at Exeter.

ASTOR HALL

Left: The King and Queen visiting Plymouth in 1942. Soon after their visit Plymouth suffered one of the worst bombings of the war.

Right: Lady Nancy Astor visiting the bombed and smoking ruins of the Church of St Andrew's. On 22 March 1941 the great church of Plymouth lay gutted by fire and incendiary bombs which had been dropped through the night. The devastation was terrible, the roof was gone and so were the furnishings and the new organ. Only the old stone walls and the tower remained and this seemed to epitomise the city motto, *Turris fortissima est nomen Jehovah.*

The Tower Window is now the Astor memorial window and the inscription reads: 'This window is in Memory of Waldorf, 2nd Viscount Astor, Member of Parliament 1910-19, Lord Mayor of Plymouth 1939-44, Freeman of the City.' The six stained-glass windows now in place in the church were all designed by John Piper and made by Patrick Reyntiens.

And below Lord and Lady Astor are seen attending one of the services held in the bombed ruins of the church. This one was held for Special Constables in August 1943.

The first bomb fell on the city at Swilly heralding the blitz that was to follow when thousands of homes were destroyed and the face of Plymouth was totally altered. During the 2nd world war 1,172 civilians were killed with over 4,448 civilian casualties; as well as the many churches, hotels, schools and public houses that were demolished, 3,754 houses had gone.

There were two direct hits on the Naval barracks but figures were never released of the service personnel who were killed or injured.

Left: St Andrew's Church from Spooner's Corner.
Above: Charles Church.

The then Mr and Mrs Winston Churchill
visiting the blitzed city of Plymouth in May
1941. 'Your homes are down but your hearts
are high', was the typically Churchillian
phrase he gave to boost the morale of
Plymothians.

Left: Nuns salvaging from the wreckage.
Below: Searching for bodies among the ruins.

Above: Surrender of a German submarine.
Left: Women demolition workers.
Below: St Andrew's Church illuminated on
Peace night.

Temporary shops which were constructed in
Nissen huts in Plymouth after the blitz of
1941. Some of these survived until after the
1950s, most of them in the area surrounding
the Guildhall.

Her Majesty the Queen, the present Queen
Mother, with the silver gilt cup which was
given by Queen Elizabeth I to Sir Francis
Drake. The cup was purchased by the
National Art Collections Fund and presented
to the Plymouth City Museum and Art
Gallery. During the War, when this
photograph was taken, the cup was put away
for safe keeping but it can now be seen in
the Plymouth Museum and Art Gallery.

Two of the street parties held in Plymouth to celebrate peace at Lower Mount Gold and Stonehouse.

Two views of the Victory Parade in 1945
marching through Plymouth.

Crowds awaiting the first post-war carnival
procession in Plymouth. The picture was
taken in Old Town Street in 1947.

The ship's company of HMS *Amethyst* marching through Plymouth on 1 November 1949 after their escape from the Yangtse River. Hundreds of small boats went out into the harbour to greet the *Amethyst* on her return to Plymouth and the ship and her company were given a tumultuous welcome much to the embarrassment of the Government who had tried to play down the affair not wanting to further strain relationships with China.

The photograph was taken in Royal Parade when it had been laid out after the war damage but before rebuilding had started.

An aerial view of the Citadel and Sutton
Pool. The picture was presented to the
Museum of Plymouth by Major Lindsay in
1965 when he was Second in Command of
the Citadel.

The scene of Sir Francis Chichester's return to Plymouth after his single-handed, round-the-world voyage in *Gypsy Moth IV*. He had covered 28,500 miles with only one stop in Sydney and had done it in record time having left Plymouth on 26 August 1966 and returning on 29 May 1967.

Sir Francis's ambition had been to sail around the world in a time comparable to the clippers of old. His voyage, unlike others before him, had been a race as well as an adventure. This endeavour of a man in his sixties caught the imagination of people all over the world.

When he sailed into Plymouth on that May evening hundreds of vessels, from the smallest dinghy to Naval mine sweepers, went out beyond the Breakwater to greet him. A salvo of three guns signalled the finish of his voyage at 8.56 p.m.

Gipsy Moth IV was escorted to her buoy at the Royal Western Yacht Club and finally Sir Francis stepped ashore at 10 p.m. in a blaze of floodlights and to the cheers of hundreds of people who had gathered on the Hoe to welcome him home. It was a day many Plymothians will long remember.

Left: Derry's Cross in festive mood.
Above: Sunset over the Sound.

ALSO AVAILABLE

VIEWS OF OLD CORNWALL
by Sarah Foot.
Nearly 200 old picture postcards from the Peter Dryden collection, with text by Sarah Foot, all combine to recall Cornwall as she once was.
'. . . will be certain to start the talk flowing of days gone by.'
The Cornishman

A CORNISH CAMERA
by George Ellis and Sarah Foot.
More than 200 photographs taken by George Ellis, the doyen of Cornish press photographers: Cornwall at work and play in war and peace; town and countryside and coast; personalities and customs; triumphs and tragedies. Sarah Foot's text adds the stories behind these pictures.

'A delightfully nostalgic look back at the last 40 years in the County'.
Sunday Independent

THE CORNISH YEAR BOOK
Over 150 photographs and drawings.
Writers, artists and photographers have all combined to reveal facets of Cornwall and a Cornish way of life through spring, summer, autumn and winter.

STRANGE STORIES FROM DEVON
by Rosemary Anne Lauder and Michael Williams. 46 photographs.
Strange shapes and places — strange characters — the man they couldn't hang, and a Salcombe mystery, the Lynmouth disaster and a mysterious house are only some of the strange stories.
'A riveting read'.
The Plymouth Times
'. . . well-written and carefully edited'
Monica Wyatt, Teignmouth Post & Gazette

DEVON MYSTERIES
by Judy Chard. 22 photographs.
Devon is not only a beautiful county, it's a mysterious place too — and if anybody had any doubts about that, Judy Chard demolishes them with her exploration into the strange and often the inexplicable. This book, though, is not just about mysterious Devon, it's essentially about Devon mysteries.
'. . . my appetite for unexplained happenings has been truly whetted by Newton Abbot author Judy Chard's latest offering.' Mid Devon Advertiser
'. . . comprehensive catalogue of strange goings-on in Devon . . .'
North Devon Journal-Herald

LEGENDS OF DEVON
by Sally Jones. 60 photographs and drawings.
Devon is a mine of folklore and myth. Here in a journey through legendary Devon, Sally Jones brings into focus some fascinating tales, showing us that the line dividing fact and legend is an intriguing one.
'. . .Sally Jones has trodden the path of legendary Devon well . . .'
Tavistock Times

DARTMOOR PRISON
by Rufus Endle. 35 photographs.
A vivid portrait of the famous prison on the moor stretching from 1808 — with rare photographs taken inside today.
'The bleak Devon cage's 170 year history . . . fascinatingly sketched by one of the Westcountry's best known journalists Rufus Endle . . . the man with the key to Dartmoor.'
Western Daily Press

VIEWS OF OLD DEVON
Rosemary Anne Lauder provides the text for more than 200 postcards, evocative of a world and a way of life that has gone.
'Only the camera can turn back the clock like this.'
The Sunday Independent

FOLLOWING THE TAMAR
by Sarah Foot. 63 photographs and map.
Sarah Foot is the Tamar's inevitable author, living only a mile from its banks, seeing it every day from her Cornish home, and truly loving it.
'. . . both a labour of love and a work of subtle selection, combining the intriguing byways of local history and geography with a profusion of well-chosen black and white plates.' Dick Benson-Gyles, The Western Evening Herald

FOLLOWING THE RIVER FOWEY
by Sarah Foot. 49 photographs.
Sarah Foot follows the Fowey from its beginnings on Bodmin Moor to where it meets the sea beyond Fowey and Polruan.
'She stitches into the simple tapestry of the river's story names and incidents and anecdotes, deftly and lovingly, every thread and every page touched with charm and an unashamed sense of delight.'
Western Morning News

CURIOSITIES OF DEVON
by Michael Williams.
Michael Williams explores strange and unusual aspects of a county of contrasts; curious customs and characters, strange architecture and landscapes, and highly individual Dartmoor characters. There are visits to the Finch Foundry at Sticklepath and Arlington Court.

MY DEVON
Ten writers writing about their Devon: Hugh Caradon, Judy Chard, Andrew Cooper, Robin Davidson, Daniel Farson, Sarah Foot, Clive Gunnell, James Mildren, Mary and Hal Price.
'. . . ten writers' impressions of their favourite places . . the personal approach warms and enlivens . . .'
Herald Express

GHOSTS OF DEVON
by Peter Underwood. 44 photographs and drawings.
Peter Underwood, President of the Ghost Club, writes of the ghostly stories that saturate the County of Devon, a land full of mystery and of ghostly lore and legend.
'Packed with photographs, this is a fascinating book.'
Herald Express

SUPERSTITION AND FOLKLORE
by Michael Williams. 44 photographs.
A survey of Westcountry Superstitions: interviews on the subject and some Cornish and Devon folklore.
'. . . the strictures that we all ignore at our peril. To help us to keep out of trouble, Mr Williams has prepared a comprehensive list.'
Frank Kempe, North Devon Journal-Herald